Animals in my Backyard

SQUIRRELS

Jordan McGill

www.av2books.com

MEDIA ENHANCED BOOKS
AV²
BY WEIGL™
ADDED VALUE • AUDIO VISUAL

Go to **www.av2books.com**, and enter this book's unique code.

BOOK CODE

C579182

AV² by Weigl brings you media enhanced books that support active learning.

AV² provides enriched content that supplements and complements this book. Weigl's AV² books strive to create inspired learning and engage young minds in a total learning experience.

Your AV² Media Enhanced books come alive with...

Audio
Listen to sections of the book read aloud.

Video
Watch informative video clips.

Embedded Weblinks
Gain additional information for research.

Try This!
Complete activities and hands-on experiments.

Key Words
Study vocabulary, and complete a matching word activity.

Quizzes
Test your knowledge.

Slide Show
View images and captions, and prepare a presentation.

... and much, much more!

Published by AV² by Weigl
350 5th Avenue, 59th Floor New York, NY 10118
Website: www.av2books.com www.weigl.com

Library of Congress Cataloging-in-Publication Data

McGill, Jordan.
  Squirrels / Jordan McGill.
    p. cm. -- (Animals in my backyard)
  ISBN 978-1-61690-931-4 (hardcover : alk. paper) -- ISBN 978-1-61913-005-0 (pbk) -- ISBN 978-1-61690-577-4 (online)
1. Squirrels--Juvenile literature. I. Title.
  QL737.R68M334 2012
  599.36--dc23
                            2011023425

Printed in the United States of America in North Mankato, Minnesota
3 4 5 6 7 8 9 0   17 16 15 14 13

082013
WEP270813

Project Coordinator: Jordan McGill Art Director: Terry Paulhus

Weigl acknowledges Getty Images as the primary image supplier for this title.

Animals in my Backyard
SQUIRRELS

CONTENTS

Meet the squirrel.

He has a big, bushy tail.

He lives with his family
while he grows.

While he grows,
he stays with his mother.

6

He keeps dry with his big tail.

With his big tail, he keeps warm.

He climbs with his sharp claws.

With his sharp claws,
he holds on to trees.

He bites things to wear down his teeth.

His teeth always grow.

He keeps his food in trees and below the ground.

Below the ground,
some of his food is hidden.

He is fast for his size.

His size helps him jump far.

He has a home up high.

Up high, he makes a bed
of fur, feathers, and moss.

If you meet the squirrel,
he might run to a tree.
Let him be.

If you meet the squirrel,
stay away.

SQUIRREL FACTS

This page provides more detail about the interesting facts found in the book.
Simply look for the corresponding page number to match the fact.

**Pages
4-5**

Meet the squirrel. Squirrels are small, common rodents. They are mammals that have a bushy tail. There are many kinds of squirrels, but tree squirrels are the most common in North America. There are also ground squirrels that burrow and live underground and flying squirrels that glide through the air.

**Pages
6–7**

Squirrel babies cannot see when they are born. They are hairless and have no teeth. The mother protects them and feeds them. At three weeks old, the babies have two teeth and some hair. By five weeks, their eyes are open. By 12 weeks, squirrels leave their mother and begin to care for themselves.

**Pages
8–9**

Squirrels use their big, fluffy tail to shield themselves from the Sun, rain, and snow. They also use their tail as a blanket to keep warm. Squirrels communicate with their tail. They wave it at other squirrels and flick it to scare off predators. Their tail can also act as a parachute if they fall.

**Pages
10–11**

Squirrels have sharp claws. They use their claws to climb trees. Their claws also help them grip thin objects such as wires and branches. A squirrel's claws let the squirrel move around in trees quickly. Squirrels like being up high because most of their predators are not good climbers. A squirrel can fall more than 100 feet (30 meters) without getting hurt.

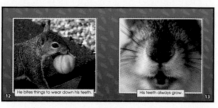

All squirrels have sharp front teeth. They use their teeth to break open nuts to eat. A squirrel's teeth grow very fast, up to 6 inches (15 centimeters) each year. Squirrels have to eat all the time and chew on hard objects, such as twigs, to shorten their teeth.

Most squirrels store food. Tree squirrels bury food in the ground, in hollow trees, or under leaves. Squirrels make an important contribution to the environment. They forget about many of the nuts, seeds, berries, and mushrooms they bury. This forgotten food grows into new plants. Sometimes, squirrels eat insects, eggs, and small animals, such as lizards and frogs.

Squirrels can run more than 10 miles (16 kilometers) per hour. One police officer claims to have clocked a squirrel running more than 20 miles (32 km) per hour. A squirrel's light weight and speed allow him to run and jump in amazing ways. Squirrels can often be seen jumping from branch to branch.

Squirrels claim a piece of land as their own. This space is called the squirrel's range. Tree squirrels live in trees. Tree squirrels make dreys, or nests, from twigs and bark. The dreys may be lined with fur, feathers, moss, grass, and dead leaves.

Most squirrels will run away if you get too close. However, some have become quite comfortable around people. If you come across a squirrel, do not feed it. It is also important not to touch a squirrel. Squirrels have sharp teeth, and they may bite. They can carry diseases that make people sick.

WORD LIST

Research has shown that as much as 65 percent of all written material published in English is made up of 300 words. These 300 words cannot be taught using pictures or learned by sounding them out. They must be recognized by sight. This book contains 41 common sight words to help young readers improve their reading fluency and comprehension. This book also teaches young readers several important content words. These words are paired with pictures to aid in learning and improve understanding.

Page	Sight Words First Appearance
4	the
5	a, big, has, he
6	family, grows, his, lives, mother, while, with
8	keeps
11	on, to, trees
12	down, things
13	always
14	and, below, food, in, the, up
15	is, of, some
16	far, helps, him, jump
18	high, home
19	makes
20	be, if, let, might, run, you

Page	Content Words First Appearance
4	squirrel
5	tail
10	claws
12	teeth
14	ground
16	size
19	bed, fur, feathers, moss

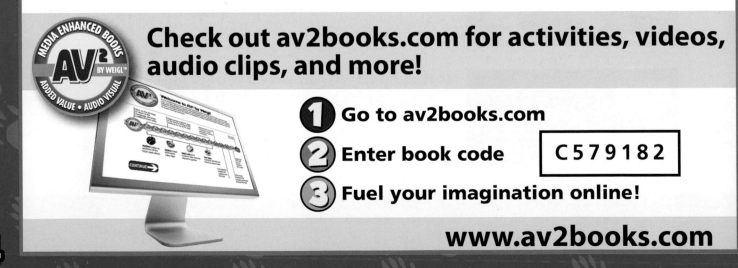

Check out av2books.com for activities, videos, audio clips, and more!

1 Go to av2books.com

2 Enter book code C 5 7 9 1 8 2

3 Fuel your imagination online!

www.av2books.com